Life in the Old West

LIFE ON THE RANCH

Bobbie Kalman

🌲 Crabtree Publishing Company

LIFE IN THE OLD WEST

Created by Bobbie Kalman

For Peter
an urban cowboy

Author and Editor-in-Chief
Bobbie Kalman

Managing editor
Lynda Hale

Senior editor
April Fast

Research and editing team
Kate Calder
John Crossingham

Computer design
Lynda Hale
Robert MacGregor (cover concept)
Campbell Creative Services

Photo research
Kate Calder

Production coordinator
Hannelore Sotzek

Special thanks to
Mary Helmich, California State Parks; Katrina Hoover and Sutter's Fort State Historic Park; Jerri Stone, National Cowboy Hall of Fame; Tanque Verde Ranch; Pioneer Arizona Living History Museum; Hugh A. Dempsey

Photographs and reproductions
American Heritage Center, University of Wyoming: page 17; Archive Photos: pages 15 (top); Castle Rock/Archive Photos: page 31; Bobbie Kalman: pages 10 (bottom), 27, 30 (top); Jerry Koontz/The Picture Cube: page 24 (bottom); Montana Historical Society, Helena: pages 24 (top), 25; Montana Historical Society, Helena/Evelyn J. Cameron: page 15 (bottom); Montana Historical Society, Helena/L.A. Huffman: pages 4, 19 (top); National Cowboy Hall of Fame, Oklahoma City: pages 11 (bottom), 12, 13; Edward Owen/Art Resource, NY (detail): page 14 (bottom); Tony & Alba Sanches-Zinnanti: page 14 (top); Inga Spence/The Picture Cube: title page, page 21 (bottom); The Stock Solution/David Stoecklein: pages 10 (top), 16, 18, 22-23, 29 (bottom); Tanque Verde Ranch: page 30 (bottom); James Walker, *Vaqueros in a Horse Corral*, 1877, collection of Gilcrease Museum, Tulsa (detail): pages 6-7; other images by Digital Vision & Image Club Graphics

Illustrations
Barbara Bedell: pages 8-9, 25, 26, 27 (top left); Bonna Rouse: back cover, pages 12, 13, 15, 27 (bottom), 28, lasso border throughout book

Crabtree Publishing Company

350 Fifth Avenue
Suite 3308
New York
N.Y. 10118

360 York Road, RR 4
Niagara-on-the-Lake
Ontario, Canada
L0S 1J0

73 Lime Walk
Headington
Oxford OX3 7AD
United Kingdom

Cataloging in Publication Data
Kalman, Bobbie
  Life on the ranch

(Life in the Old West)
Includes index.

ISBN 0-7787-0071-2 (library bound) ISBN 0-7787-0103-4 (pbk.)
This book examines the various aspects of nineteenth century cattle ranching, including the work of the ranchers and cowboys, the food and living arrangements, and the influence of the Spanish cowboys.

1. Ranching—West (North America)—History—19th century—Juvenile literature. 2. Ranch life—West (North America)—History—19th century—Juvenile literature. [1. Ranch life—West (North America)] I. Title. II. Series: Kalman, Bobbie. Life in the Old West.

SF197.5.K36 1999   j636'.01'097809034   LC 98-42366
                                                        CIP

TABLE OF CONTENTS

Ranching in the West 4

Sheep Ranches 6

Around the Ranch 8

Ranchers and Cowboys 12

Women on the Ranch 14

Jobs at the Ranch 16

Out on the Range 18

The Horses 20

A Day on the Ranch 22

Fun and Community Life 24

Ranch Tools and Clothing 26

Threats to the Ranch 28

Dude Ranches 30

Glossary 31

Index 32

Ranching in the West

By the mid 1800s, thousands of settlers moved west to start **ranches**. Land in the west was cheap or given away free. The cities in the east were growing larger, and people needed more food, especially meat. Ranchers saw the demand for beef as an opportunity to make money. Many of the first ranches were small, but some grew into huge businesses.

Cattle on the open range

Millions of cattle roamed the unsettled land in the west, called the **open range**. The ranchers claimed the cattle and **branded**, or marked them with the symbol of their ranch. Cattle from many different ranches grazed on the open range and drank from the streams. Cowboys were hired to look after the cattle and round them up.

From the west to the east

The cowboys gathered the cattle and **drove**, or guided, them hundreds of miles along trails. The cattle had to walk to a **cattle town**, or town with a railroad station, where they were sold. They were put on railway cars heading east. Before long, the railways extended farther west, making it easier to transport cattle.

The spread of ranching

By the late 1800s, ranching had become a profitable business, and some ranchers owned thousands of acres of land. Between 1865 and 1885, ranchers had sold more than 10 million cattle and hired over 40,000 cowboys. New ranches were established in the northwestern states and western Canada.

THE FIRST RANCHES

The word ranch comes from the Spanish word *rancho*. The first ranches in North America were owned by the Spanish. The Spanish came to this continent in the 1500s and claimed Mexico and the region stretching from Texas to California. They called these territories New Spain.

Until the Spanish arrived, there were no horses or cattle in North America. The Spanish brought hundreds of horses and longhorn cattle with them. The animals grazed in the wild and quickly grew in number. The Spanish sold the hide and **tallow**, or fat, of the cattle, which was used to make candles and soap.

The *vaqueros*

When the early American ranchers came to the west, the Spanish were still there. They taught the newcomers how to be cowboys. Spanish-speaking cowboys were called *vaqueros*. The *vaqueros* showed the American ranchers how to tame horses and herd and rope cattle. The cowboys also copied the equipment and clothing of the *vaqueros*. They started using western saddles and ropes called **lariats**. They wore wide-brimmed hats and leather pant protectors called **chaps**.

AROUND THE RANCH

Large ranches had many different buildings. There was a home for the rancher, a home for the cowboys, and barns for storing and repairing equipment. These buildings were usually built near a stream or a clear lake. Fresh water was used for cooking, cleaning, and drinking.

The rancher and his family lived in the **main house**, or ranch house. It was the biggest and best-looking building on the ranch. Successful ranchers had large homes that were two stories high. They were well decorated and furnished. The home was used for entertaining guests.

The bunkhouse

The cowboys lived in the **bunkhouse**, which was one large room with a dirt or wooden floor. A bunkhouse was an untidy place with bedbugs and lice. It was not comfortable, but it was home to the cowboys. Inside were beds, tables, and chairs. The walls were covered with old newspaper to keep out the wind and rain. Buffalo or wolf skins were hung on the walls to provide extra warmth.

Corral

The **corral** was located close to the stables. It was a fenced area in which horses were kept and trained. The wooden fence was built to form a large circle so the horses would not crowd into corners and hurt themselves. The round shape also helped the cowboys train the horses. It was easier to turn and ride an untamed, bucking horse in a round corral.

The mess hall

The cook above is clanging a rod on a metal triangle to call the cowboys into the **mess hall** for dinner. The mess hall, or cook house, was a small building where meals were prepared and eaten. It was beside the bunkhouse. A roof or **tarpaulin** sometimes joined the two buildings. Cowboys hung their ropes and stored their bridles in the small covered space between the bunkhouse and mess hall.

Blacksmith building

Horseshoes and ranch equipment such as farming tools, cooking utensils, and barrel hoops were made and repaired in the blacksmith building.

The blacksmith heated iron over a fire and bent it into shape with a hammer.

Stables

The horses were kept in the stables. The stables had stalls or pens where the horses slept. Each stall had a water barrel and was **bedded**, or laid with hay.

The hay and straw shed

Horses ate hay and slept on straw. Hay and straw were kept in a large open shed so they would stay dry. A cowboy cleaned out the horse stalls each day and took fresh hay and straw from the shed to the stables.

Windmills and water

Many ranches had wells that provided water for the people and animals. The water was drawn out of the ground by a pump that was powered by a windmill. The water from the well was stored in a large water tank.

(below) This ranch has a large, two-story main house. Most ranches had only men living on them, but there are several girls and women in this ranch family.

Orchards and gardens

Many ranches had orchards and gardens for growing fruits and vegetables. Ranch families were often too far from town to buy fresh fruits and vegetables, so they grew their own produce.

RANCHERS AND COWBOYS

The rancher owned the ranch and all the horses and cattle on it. He hired cowboys to help him with the animals. Some ranchers had worked as ranch hands themselves before starting their own ranches. Many were settlers from the east who traveled west to start a new life. Ranching was a tough and risky business. The land in the west was rough, and harsh weather could kill herds of cattle. Rustlers, who stole a rancher's cattle, were a constant threat. Many ranchers lost money and went out of business.

Cattle barons

Wealthy ranchers who owned huge areas of land and thousands of cattle were known as **cattle barons**. Many cattle barons were businessmen. Some had never lived on a ranch or performed any ranch work such as roping or driving cattle. Cattle barons often had other businesses as well, such as newspapers, banks, or stores.

The homes of new ranchers were often small. They built large, main houses once their ranches became profitable.

Who were the cowboys?

Thousands of young men were attracted to cowboy life. Some came from eastern cities in search of adventure and freedom. Others had grown up on ranches and already knew how to rope and herd cattle. They hoped to learn as much about ranching as possible so they could save their money and have a ranch of their own one day.

Not an easy ride!

The life of a cowboy was often lonely and difficult. Ranch work was not easy! Ranch hands worked 18-hour days, seven days a week. Their bunkhouse had a leaky roof as well as mice and rats, but few cowboys complained. They were proud to be part of a ranching business. For their hard work, they earned between 30 and 40 dollars a month.

Different backgrounds

Cowboys came from different cultures. Many were British and European settlers. Some African Americans became cowboys after they were freed from slavery. Mexican cowboys, or *vaqueros*, were descendants of the Spanish, the first ranchers in North America. Other cowboys came from Native North American heritages. Mexican, African American, and Native North American men made up one-third of all the cowboys.

Large ranches had dozens of cowboys who worked on the ranch year round. Some of these cowboys hoped to have a ranch of their own someday. Few cowboys had wives or children, so the men became one big family.

WOMEN ON THE RANCH

Most of the ranches in the west were owned by men. There were very few women on the ranches, but they had many tasks and responsibilities. They baked bread, made butter, mended clothing, and looked after the children. Women worked hard to feed and clothe their family. They also helped run the ranching business. They kept track of the cattle and equipment that was bought and sold. They looked after the money and paid the ranch hands. When extra help was needed, women rode the range, herded cattle, and did other "cowboy" jobs.

Women spent their evenings mending clothes or spinning fleece into yarn. The yarn was knitted or woven into cloth, which was used to make clothing for the family. The leftover scraps of cloth were used to weave rag rugs. During the day, women were busy cooking and baking, doing laundry, making candles, and churning butter.

Women's work

Some women helped thresh and bale hay for the stables. They watered the horses and cleaned out the stables. They worked side by side with the men, helping them brand the animals and herd the cattle. They did rough cowhand work that people in the east considered "unsuitable" for women.

Hard-working girls

Girls worked hard on the ranch, too. Older girls helped their mother tend the vegetable garden. They sewed, cooked, and did laundry. The younger girls fed the chickens, milked the cows, and collected eggs. Some young girls learned how to use a **lariat**, or rope.

Women who spent most of their time doing ranch jobs became expert cattle herders. They owned their own saddle, lariat, and cowboy hat and wore comfortable cowboy clothing.

(top) These two young "cowhands" learned to ride soon after they learned to walk. (bottom) Women often helped care for the animals on the ranch.

Large cattle ranches needed many people to take care of the land, equipment, and animals. The ranchers hired cowboys to work during the spring, summer, fall, and sometimes the winter. There were many chores to be done. Smaller ranches had only a few cowboys who did all the chores, but larger ranches had dozens of cowboys. Each did specific jobs.

Grub-line riders

Some cowboys rode on horseback from ranch to ranch working as **grub-line riders**. Grub-line riders did odd jobs such as tending animals and making repairs around a ranch. Ranchers paid them with a meal and a place to sleep. Grub-line riders brought ranchers news from other ranches and often told entertaining stories.

The cook

The cook was often an old, retired cowboy who prepared the meals for the other cowboys. He usually slept in the mess hall and was a permanent member of the ranch. Sometimes the cook also supervised the ranch hands. He was the closest thing to a doctor on the ranch. He looked after sick or injured cowboys.

Dangers on the ranch

Working on the ranch was dangerous! Cowboys could fall from a high windmill or steep barn roof that they were fixing. Cattle with long horns sometimes stabbed cowboys who were not careful. If a cowboy was stabbed by a cow or kicked by a wild horse, the cook did his best to bandage him. There were few medical doctors in the west!

Cowboy jobs

* repairing fences and putting up new ones
* gathering and chopping firewood
* fixing buildings
* repairing windmills
* cleaning the horse stables
* looking after sick or pregnant animals
* milking the cows
* making sure the animals had enough to eat and drink
* melting **suet**, or cattle fat, into **tallow** for making candles and soap

(opposite page) In the summer, the cowboys were busy harvesting hay. They stored the hay and used it over the long winter to feed the animals on the ranch.

Out on the Range

The main work of cattle ranching was raising cattle so they could be sold for their beef. The cattle grazed on the open range or on a rancher's land. It took many cowboys to look after the cattle and make sure they were healthy and ready to be sold.

Taking care of the cattle

Cowboys had to keep a close eye on the cattle on the open range. They brought back sick or pregnant cattle to the ranch so the ranch hands could care for them. They rescued cattle that were stuck in thick mud at watering holes.

Blowflies were bugs that infected cattle on the open range. The bugs landed in open wounds, such as fresh brand marks, and laid eggs.

The eggs hatched into small **screwworms** that were painful to the cattle and sometimes killed them. Cowboys made their own medicines to kill the worms, but the medicines often made the cattle even sicker!

Line riders

Line riders were cowboys who rode for miles around the ranch. They watched for stray cattle, guarded the cattle against rustlers, and hunted the wolves that preyed on cattle. A line rider also told the rancher when grazing land was dry and sparse or watering holes and pastures were frozen over. In the winter, line riders often led animals lost in blizzards back to the ranch. They helped clear snow and ice off watering holes so the cattle could drink.

Line camps

Some ranchers set up shelters called **line camps** every few miles on the outskirts of the ranch property. Line riders could rest, eat, and warm up at the line camps. In the summer, the air and land became hot and dry, so line riders at the camps kept a close watch for prairie fires.

Ready to go!

Cattle were branded with the symbol of the ranch so that ranchers would know to which ranch the animals belonged. The cattle that were ready to be sold were **rounded up**, or gathered. Cowboys then drove the animals to cattle towns, which were often hundreds of miles away. The cattle were sold and put on railway cars heading east.

(above) Cowboys on the range gather for lunch at this line camp. The cook has prepared a hardy meal.

(below) Rounding up the cattle was a big job. The cattle wandered far from the ranch and were often wild after spending months on the range. Roping them was difficult and dangerous.

THE HORSES

Horses were a very important part of cattle ranching. They were used to herd cattle, pull wagons, and perform other heavy farm work. The cowboys on the range rode their horse all day. Ranchers also used horses to make trips to neighboring ranches or to the nearest town.

Wild broncos

Bronco busters captured **broncos**, or wild horses, and brought them back to the ranch to **break**, or tame. Bronco busters broke the horses in the corral. The broncos were not used to being in a corral and certainly not used to being ridden. They would kick, turn, and buck, sending the cowboy to the ground with a thump. Bronco busters were rough with the horses and used spurs and a **quirt**, or whip, to control them

Keeping the horses healthy

Horses that were already broken had to be checked for diseases. Cowboys also examined the hoofs of the horses regularly to make sure that their horseshoes were still in good shape. Horses that needed new shoes were shod.

A Day on the Ranch

My name is Jimmy, and I work for the Double Diamond ranch in Texas. Every day I roll out of bed just as the sun is coming up over the horizon and start a full day's work on the ranch. This morning I was plenty tired, but the smell of the bacon and coffee that the cook was preparing got me out of bed quickly.

After I ate my breakfast, I saddled up my horse, Old Paint, and headed out onto the range with the other ranch hands to finish the last of the fall roundup.

My friend Tom and I had to pull a cow out of a mud hole. First we threw our lariats around her neck and then tied our ropes to the horn of our saddle. It took all the strength our horses had to pull the cow out.

When we finally got her out of the mud, she was mighty mad. She charged and sent us running! After the last of the cattle had been rounded up and the ranch hands had eaten some sourdough biscuits and coffee, we spent the afternoon branding cattle.

It was my job to separate the small calves from their mothers so they could be branded. This was a challenge! The calves stay so close to their mothers that I had to ride my horse between them to split them apart. One mother cow got so mad after I had roped her calf, that she came after me as I was dragging the calf to the branding pit. My horse narrowly escaped her blunt horns and got so excited that it nearly threw me off.

We finished branding the last calf, but there was still work to be done before supper.

The other ranch hands and I chopped piles of wood that we'll need during the coming winter. I was sure hungry when dinnertime came! The cook made son-of-a-gun stew and more sourdough biscuits. I gobbled it all up and then had a second helping.

After dinner, I went back to the bunkhouse with the other ranch hands. Some of the men played checkers. I read the newspaper that we pasted up on the wall to keep out the cold wind at night. Finally, it was time to put out the lantern's flame and go sleep. I fell sound asleep the minute my head hit the pillow.

Although there was a lot of tiring work to do on a ranch, the ranchers and cowboys took time to have fun. Cowboys spent much of their time in the bunkhouses. They passed the time by playing card games, checkers, and dominoes. During these games, they gambled for money. Gambling was not allowed on most ranches, but many cowboys broke the rules and made bets anyway.

Music

Music brought the ranch to life. Some ranches had a piano in the main house, which was played by the rancher's wife and children. Music from guitars, fiddles, and harmonicas came from the bunkhouse, accompanied by clapping and stomping sounds. If the cowboys had no instruments, they sang or hummed the songs.

Cowboy mischief

Sometimes cowboys could not resist getting into mischief. Often they tried to ride an oxen, mule, or cow. These animals would buck or run around trying to get the cowboy off their back. Cowboys also raced one another on fast horses and made bets on who would win.

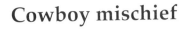

Bull-riding competitions are now a big part of rodeos.

Special occasions

On special occasions such as a wedding, the rancher invited the cowboys to the main house for a dance. Cowboys and families from other ranches spent the night dancing. Everyone dressed in their best clothing. The ladies wore their Sunday dresses and high-buttoned shoes, and the men wore clean white shirts. They even shined their boots!

RANCH TOOLS AND CLOTHING

Herding, roping, and branding were tasks that were unique to life on the ranch. Cowboys needed tools such as branding irons and strong hand-braided ropes. This equipment could not be bought in stores. The blacksmith and the cowboys made these necessary tools.

Lariats
Cowboys used lariats to catch and handle horses and cattle on the ranch. Lariats were braided ropes made from tough hemp fibers. Hemp ropes were strong, stiff, and easy to throw at a moving target.

Branding irons
A branding iron was a tool that was used to create a mark in an animal's hide. Each ranch had a different mark that they branded onto their animals. Brands helped the ranchers identify the animals that belonged to them. The blacksmith made the branding iron by heating up and bending metal into a symbol. The symbol was attached to a metal rod. To brand an animal, the branding iron was held over an open fire and then pressed against an animal's hide to form a permanent mark.

horn

cantle

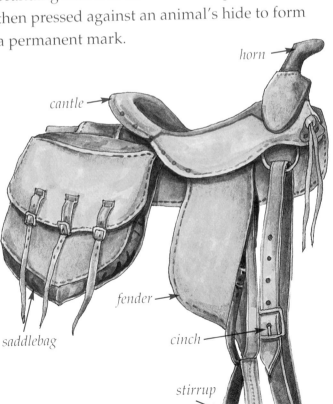

fender

saddlebag

cinch

stirrup

Saddles
A saddle was a cowboy's most important piece of equipment. Saddles kept a cowboy secure and comfortable on a horse's back. The straps of leather that hung from the saddle were used for attaching equipment such as lariats and bedrolls. Saddlebags were also used to carry extra equipment. When a cowboy roped an animal, he tied the end of the lariat to the horn on the front of the saddle.

Cowboy hat

A wide-brimmed hat protected a cowboy's face from the sun, wind, and rain. A cowboy also used his hat for bringing water to his horse or for fanning a fire.

Spurs

Cowboys wore spurs on their boots. Spurs were round, pointed disks attached to the heel of the boot. The cowboy tapped his horse gently with the spurs to get the horse moving. Some spurs also had bells called **jinglebobs** attached to them. The jingling noise made the horse move, and cowboys liked the gentle sound.

Many cowboys were proud of their decorative spurs. Others felt that a skilled rider did not have to use spurs to control a horse.

Bandannas

Bandannas were worn around a cowboy's neck and could be tied over his mouth and nose to keep him from breathing dust and dirt. A bandanna could be used as a bandage if a cowboy was cut or injured. Cowboys could also pour dirty water through their bandanna to strain it before drinking.

Cowboy boots

Cowboy boots were made to help a cowboy ride on horseback, but they were not comfortable for walking. The toes were pointed for slipping easily into the stirrups of the saddle. The high heels kept a cowboy's feet from slipping through the stirrups. The soles were thin, so a cowboy could feel the stirrups under his feet. The stitching on the side of the boot kept the leather stiff and strong.

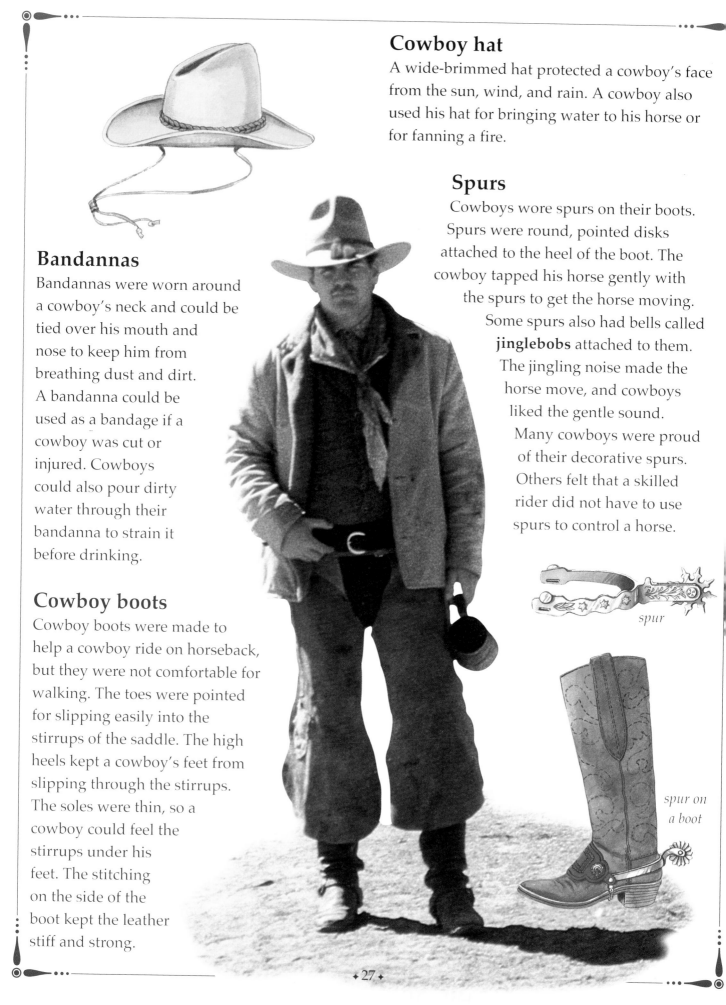

spur

spur on a boot

THREATS TO THE RANCH

Ranchers depended on their cattle to make it through the winter safely so they could be taken to market and sold. Although some cowboys spent the winter patrolling the range, it was impossible for them to keep an eye on all the cattle. They had to worry about the cattle being attacked by wild animals. Cattle were eaten by wild animals, such as wolves, mountain lions, eagles, and grizzly bears.

Rustlers were a common threat to a ranch. They stole young cattle that had not yet been branded and put their own brand on them. Sometimes they stole branded cattle and changed the brands with their own branding irons. Some rustlers even raided the ranch buildings and stole horses. Ranchers lost money and risked losing their ranch when their livestock was stolen.

Cold temperatures and raging blizzards could kill cattle. In cold weather, cattle became weak and unable to find food in the snow. They often stood helpless in a deep snowdrift, freezing and starving to death. In the winter of 1886-87, more than three-quarters of all the cattle in the west were killed by blizzards. Many ranchers lost all their cattle and went out of business.

Homesteaders and fences

More and more **homesteaders**, or settlers, began moving to the west from the eastern states. Their land was part of what was once the open range, where the cattle grazed. Some of the homesteaders built ranches. Others built farms for growing crops. Farmers did not want cattle roaming on their land, so they put up barbed-wire fences.

Range wars

Cattle ranchers tried to force the homesteaders to move away by hurting their sheep or cutting their fences. Some ranchers put up their own fences over homesteader property. Homesteaders were angry that cattle ranchers were hoarding the land that didn't really belong to them. They fought back by cutting ranch fences. Fence cutting caused fights that sometimes resulted in ranch buildings being destroyed or a rancher being hurt or killed.

DUDE RANCHES

Although the days of driving cattle thousands of miles along a wide open trail are over, people interested in living the life of a cowboy can take a vacation on a **dude ranch**. On a dude ranch, vacationers from cities, or **dudes**, learn how to saddle and ride horses, rope cattle, and camp out on the open range like the cowboys of the old west. Some dude ranches even give lessons on how to shoe horses and round up cattle.

Real cowboy work

Many of today's dude ranches are real working ranches. They use the help of vacationers in mending fences, branding cattle, and driving them to different grazing pastures.

Glossary

barbed wire Fence wire that has sharp points

branding The act of marking an animal's hide

bridle A harness made out of leather straps that is put on a horse's head in order to control the horse

bronco buster A cowboy who tames wild horses

cattle town A town with a railway station where thousands of cattle were driven to be sold

dude ranch A ranch where vacationers can spend time learning how to do cowboy jobs

grub-line riders Cowboys who rode from ranch to ranch in winter doing odd jobs in exchange for room and board

line camps Shacks located around the ranch where the cowboys rested, ate, and warmed themselves

line riders Cowboys who rode around the outskirts of a ranch to look after the cattle and guard them from rustlers

mess hall A large room with tables and chairs where the cowboys ate their meals

open range A large area of open, unsettled land on which a rancher's cattle grazed, or fed

ranch A farm where cattle are raised

roundup An event in which cattle were gathered from the open range in order to be taken on a cattle drive

rustlers People who stole cattle

settlers Men and women who built homes on the open land

tarpaulin A large sheet of material used for protection from harsh weather

vaqueros Spanish or Mexican cowboys

windmills Wooden towers with round, fanlike wheels at the top that are turned by the wind and used to power water pumps

Index

African Americans 13

bandannas 27

barns 8, 17

beef 4, 18

blacksmith 10, 26

blizzards 18, 28

branding 4, 15, 19, 22, 23, 26, 28, 30

bridle 10

broncos 21

bunkhouse 9, 10, 13, 23, 24

cattle 4, 5, 6, 7, 12, 13, 14, 15, 16, 17, 18, 19, 20, 22, 23, 24, 26, 28, 29, 30

cattle baron 12

cattle drive 12, 19, 30

cattle thieves 12, 18, 28

cities 4, 13

clothes 7, 14, 15, 25, 26-27

cook 10, 17, 19, 22, 23

cooking 8, 10, 14, 15, 17, 19

corral 9, 21

cowboys 4, 5, 7, 8, 9, 10, 11, 12-13, 16, 17, 18, 19, 20, 21, 24, 25, 26, 27, 30

dangers 12, 17, 18, 19, 21 22, 23, 28-29

doctors 17

dude ranches 30

entertainment 16, 23, 24-25

fall 16, 22

families 8, 11, 13, 14, 24, 25

fences 9, 17, 29, 30

food 4, 10, 11, 14, 15, 16, 17, 19, 22, 23

grazing 4, 6, 18, 29, 30

herding 7, 13, 14, 15, 20, 26

horses 6, 7, 9, 11, 12, 15, 16, 17, 20-21, 22, 23, 24, 26, 27, 28, 30

horseshoes 10, 21, 30

jobs 9, 12, 13, 14, 15, 16-17, 19, 20, 22-23

main house 8, 11, 12, 25

medicine 18

mess hall 10, 17

Mexicans 13

money 4, 12, 13, 14, 24, 28

Native North Americans 13

open range 4, 14, 18-19, 20, 22, 28, 29, 30

railway 5, 19

ranch buildings 8-11, 17, 28, 29

ranchers 4, 5, 7, 8, 12-13, 16, 18, 19, 20, 24, 25, 26, 28, 29

ranch hands 12, 14, 17, 18, 22, 23

ropes 7, 10, 15, 22, 26

roping 7, 12, 13, 19, 23, 26, 30

roundup 19, 22, 30

saddles 15, 22, 26, 27, 30

settlers 4, 12, 13, 29

Spanish 6, 7, 13

spring 16

spurs 21, 27

stables 9, 11, 15, 17

summer 16, 17, 19

tools 10, 26-27, 28

trail 5, 30

vaqueros 7, 13

water 8, 11, 15, 18, 27

weather 9, 12

windmill 11, 17

winter 16, 17, 18, 23, 28

women 11, 13, 14-15, 24

1 2 3 4 5 6 7 8 9 0   Printed in the U.S.A.   7 6 5 4 3 2 1 0 9 8